OX

D0787207

EUREKA!
I've discovered
HEAT

Todd Plummer

mc Marshall Cavendish
Benchmark
New York

Marshall Cavendish Benchmark
99 White Plains Road
Tarrytown, NY 10591
www.marshallcavendish.us

All Internet addresses were available and accurate when this book went to press.

Library of Congress Cataloging-in-Publication Data
Brent, Lynnette R., 1965-
I've discovered heat! / by Lynette Brent.
p. cm. -- (Eureka!)
Includes bibliographical references and index.
ISBN 978-0-7614-3196-1
1. Heat--Juvenile literature. I. Title.
QC256.B74 2009
536--dc22
2008014539

t=top, tr=top right, tl=top left, bl= bottom left, br=bottom right, b=bottom
Cover: Q2A Media Art Bank
Half Title : Kameel4u/ Shutterstock
Kameel4u/ Shutterstock: P7bl; Alexander Hafemann/ Istockphoto: P7mr; William Fuller/
Istockphoto: P8; Domen Colja/ Shutterstock: P11; Hd Connelly/Shutterstock: P11m; Stillfx/
Shutterstock: P11tr; PhotoSky 4t com/ Shutterstock: P15; Damomz/ Bigstockphoto: P15tr;
Harper's New Monthly Magazine: P16; Manuel/ Shutterstock: P19; Tomasz Trojanowski/
Shutterstock: P23; Samuel Acosta/Shutterstock: P27br; Magann / Dreamstime.com: P27bl;
Khafizov Ivan Harisovich/Shutterstock: P27ml; Q2AMedia Art Bank: P28-29.
Illustrations: Q2AMedia Art Bank

Created by Q2AMedia
Creative Director: Simmi Sikka
Series Editor: Jessica Cohn
Art Director: Sudakshina Basu
Designer: Mansi Mittal
Illustrators: Amit Tayal, Aadil Ahmed Siddiqui, Sanyogita Lal,
Pooja Shukla, Kusum Kala
Photo research: Sejal Sehgal
Senior Project Manager: Ravneet Kaur
Project Manager: Shekhar Kapur

Printed in Malaysia

135642

Contents

What Is Heat?

Our universe is made of matter and energy. All the "stuff" you see around you is matter. **Atoms** and **molecules**, which are too small to see with your eyes, make up matter. Energy makes the atoms and molecules in matter move. Sometimes the molecules bump into one another. Sometimes they move back and forth. The motion of these atoms and molecules creates a form of energy called **heat**. The more quickly matter moves, the more heat gets made. Even if you traveled to the coldest part of deep space, you would still find moving matter. Any bit of moving matter causes a tiny amount of heat.

Many kinds of energy can be turned into heat energy. Have you ever started jumping up and down when you're cold? Jumping creates energy—and that energy creates heat!

What is heat made of? For years, scientists believed that heat was a fluid that could move from place to place. Benjamin Thompson was among the first to prove this **theory** untrue.

Heat acts like a fluid sometimes, yet it is quite different from a fluid.

Meet Benjamin Thompson (Count Rumford)

Benjamin Thompson (1753–1814) was born in America. He worked at a factory where holes were being drilled in cannons. He noticed that when there was friction, or rubbing, on the metal, the cannons stayed hot. The metal of the cannon itself did not hold much heat. The heat came from the friction. This discovery led to a new way of thinking about heat. Thompson, also known as Count Rumford, created or helped create many items used today. He invented smokeless chimneys, thermal underwear, and a special coffee pot.

Which Takes Up More Space: Hot or Cold Air?

You Will Need:

Balloon   Nonmetal tape measure   Black felt tip marker   Freezer

1 Blow up the balloon. Tie it shut, so the air molecules cannot escape and no more air can get inside.

2 With the marker, place a dot in the middle of the balloon.

3 Use the tape measure to measure the distance around the balloon. Start and end at the dot, to show the amount of space the molecules inside are taking up.

4 Place the balloon in the freezer. Measure it again after thirty minutes. Cooled air molecules do not move as quickly, and they take up less space.

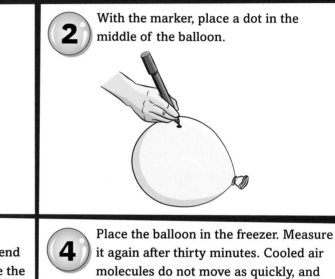

5 Place the balloon in direct sunlight. Measure it again after thirty minutes. When molecules are heated, they expand and move quickly. So they take up more space.

6 Try This: If sunlight doesn't heat up the molecules in the balloon, try placing the balloon in a pan of warm—not hot—water. (Hot water can burst the balloon and burn your skin.)

WHO WOULD HAVE THOUGHT?

What do you think of when you hear the word heat? You might think of heat as a number—as a **temperature**. A doctor will read your body temperature with a thermometer, to see if it's in the normal range. That number is a measure of the body's ability to create and get rid of heat. It's true that a higher temperature means "more heat." Yet it is more exact to say that temperature rises when **particles** in a substance move more quickly. When body temperature rises, blood vessels are moving heat to the surface of the skin. You sweat to release the heat.

Heat on the Move

Another word for move is *transfer*. Heat almost always transfers from hotter objects to cooler objects. Some materials transfer heat more easily than others. Heat transfer happens in three ways: **conduction, convection,** and **radiation.**

Convection is heat transfer by the movement of warmed matter. Cold matter sinks and warm rises. The warm matter then cools and sinks again. So it forms a cycle. Picture macaroni bobbing up and down in boiling water. You can't see heat, but you can see its movement. Conduction is heat transfer from one particle to another. A metal spoon feels somewhat cool when you take it from a drawer. The metal isn't really cold, but your hands are warmer. Heat goes from your hands to the metal.

Temperature is a measure of heat. Daniel Fahrenheit (1686–1736), a German scientist, was the first to make a **thermometer** that measured heat exactly. He formed a glass thermometer with mercury inside. Liquid mercury expands with heat, so the mercury rose as the temperature rose. The temperature scale he created to measure that rise still has his name: Fahrenheit.

So 98° is quite hot!

Meet Anders Celsius

Anders Celsius (1701–1744) was a Swedish scientist who made a thermometer soon after Fahrenheit did. Celsius's thermometer was divided into 100 degrees. He made 0 the freezing point of water at sea level. He made 100 the boiling point of water at sea level. That is the point between low and high tide. It is as close to flat on Earth as possible, so it is used for measurements. Celsius thought a scale from 0 to 100 would be easier for people to use and understand. He seems to have been right. Today, many scientists measure temperature in degrees Celsius, and many countries use the Celsius scale instead of the Fahrenheit scale.

NOW, THAT'S HOT!

How Do Thunderstorms Work?

You Will Need:

4 clear, empty soda bottles

2 index cards

Blue and red food coloring from a grocery store

Warm and cold water

 1 Fill two bottles to the brim with warm water and the other two with cold water. Use coloring to make the warm water red and the cold water blue. The red represents warm air in the atmosphere. The blue shows cold air in the atmosphere.

 2 Go outside or work over a sink or bathtub. Place an index card atop one of the bottles with warm water. Hold a hand firmly against the index card. Then turn the bottle upside down.

3 Place the mouth of that bottle on top of the mouth of one of the bottles with cold water. Keep the index card between the two bottles. Now slide the index card out from between the two bottles. What happens?

4 Repeat steps 2 and 3, but this time, place the bottle of cold water atop the bottle of warm water. Where does the warm water stay? Where does the cold water stay? Think about how that might show how warm air and cold air act when they meet.

Who Would Have Thought?

Different materials have different abilities to conduct heat. Trees and plastic tend to stay cool longer than metal. **Concrete** doesn't conduct heat well. That makes concrete a good choice for building roads and other structures. It doesn't get too hot for cars to drive on or for people to touch it. Gases such as oxygen conduct very little, if any, heat. Diamond, silver, copper, and gold are among the materials that do conduct heat. That's why copper wire is often used in machines. Heat energy can travel along the wires.

Radiation and Beyond

Convection and conduction are two ways that heat transfers through materials. Yet when you feel warm in the Sun, there is another reason for the warmth: radiation. Radiation is how heat is transferred from the Sun to Earth. On a sunny day, the energy waves from the Sun travel to Earth. Those waves warm the planet—and everything on it.

The Fahrenheit and Celsius scales do a good job of measuring outside temperatures. You might think that having two different ways to measure temperature is enough. Yet temperatures inside Earth, in space, and elsewhere can be much more extreme. So in 1848, the scientist William Thompson took the work of Fahrenheit and Celsius one step further to create the Kelvin scale. If he could explain it to you . . .

$$\triangle u^{*}(x^{*}) = \frac{R^{n+2}}{|x^{*}|^{n+2}}(\triangle u)^{*}(x^{*})$$

$$x^{*} = \frac{R^{2}}{|x|^{2}}x$$

$$x^{*} = \frac{R^{2}}{|x|^{2}}x$$

$$f^{*}(x^{*}) = \frac{|x|^{n-2}}{R^{2n-4}}f(x) = \frac{1}{|x^{*}|^{n-2}}f(x)$$

$$f^{*}(x^{*}) = \frac{|x|^{n-2}}{R^{2n-4}}f(x) = \frac{1}{|x^{*}|^{n-2}}f(x)$$

$$f^{*}(x^{*}) = \frac{|x|^{n-2}}{R^{2n-4}}f(x) = \frac{1}{|x^{*}|^{n-2}}f(x)$$

$$\triangle u^{*}(x^{*}) = \frac{R^{n+2}}{|x^{*}|^{n+2}}(\triangle u)$$

$$x^{*} = \frac{R^{2}}{|x|^{2}}x$$

Meet William Thompson (Baron Kelvin)

William Thompson (1824–1907) was a professor in Glasgow, Scotland. He had a hand in a number of scientific advances. Not only did he make a new temperature scale, but he helped people think about heat in new ways. He was instrumental in laying the first undersea cable across the Atlantic Ocean, too. Queen Victoria knighted him after that! Baron Kelvin was wrong about air travel: He famously said it wouldn't happen. But he was right about much more than he was wrong. He worked on many projects involving heat and electricity and communications.

OK! I WAS WRONG.

Why did I make a newer temperature scale?

My scale is better able to measure extreme hot and cold.

On my scale, absolute zero is the temperature at which molecules do not move at all.

On the Celsius scale, this same temperature is −273.15 degrees.

The Kelvin uses 100 degrees, much like Celsius does.

Yet Kelvin 0 is much colder than Celsius 0!

Temperature in Fahrenheit	Celsius	Kelvin
70 degrees: a warm day	21.1	294.3
32 degrees: water's freezing point	0	273.2

Make a Thermometer

You Will Need:

1/2 cup water (more as needed)

1/2 cup rubbing alcohol, used only with supervision

Clear, 12-ounce, narrow-necked plastic soda or water bottle

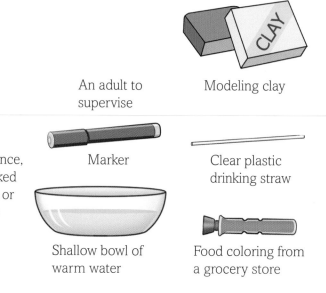

An adult to supervise

Modeling clay

Marker

Clear plastic drinking straw

Shallow bowl of warm water

Food coloring from a grocery store

Note: This experiment must be set up correctly, with the help of an adult. Do not use rubbing alcohol anywhere near a fire or flame, such as a candle or a gas burner. Do not drink the rubbing alcohol or get it in your mouth; it can make you sick. Wear safety glasses to keep the alcohol from splashing into your eyes.

1 Pour 1/2 cup water and 1/2 cup rubbing alcohol in the bottle. Color the liquid with a few drops of food dye.

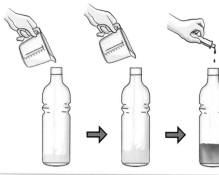

2 Insert the straw so that it rests under the surface of the liquid but does not touch the bottle's bottom. With the clay, create an airtight seal around the bottle's neck and the straw, or the thermometer will not work. Observe the level of liquid in the straw.

3 Place the homemade thermometer in the bowl of warm water. After a few minutes, observe the level of the liquid again. The mixture in the bottle expanded when warmed. This made the colored mixture move up through the straw.

4 Test what happens if the thermometer is in a shadow or in sunlight. What happens to your thermometer when it gets colder? Does wind affect the thermometer?

14

WHO WOULD HAVE THOUGHT?

Would you want to sit in a black chair in the backyard on a hot day? Probably not! When heat is radiated toward Earth, not every object warms up to the same temperature. Why not? One factor is color. Different colors **absorb** heat differently. The color black absorbs all colors of light. Absorbed light is turned into heat, so a black object becomes really warm in sunlight. The color white **reflects** light, so white doesn't absorb heat as quickly as black. If you're outside on a hot day, white is a good color choice for clothing.

Heat Changes

In science, the word law explains an action or a set of actions. Laws that relate to heat are called laws of **thermodynamics.**

The first law of thermodynamics says that energy cannot be created or destroyed. Energy can be transferred, though. If you hold an ice cube, what happens? The heat flows from you to the ice, causing the ice to melt. Heat transfers from the hand to ice, yet the total amount of heat between the two is always the same.

The second law says that **entropy**, or disorder, tends to increase. What does this mean? In practical terms, if you add heat energy to something, the energy tends to spread out. If you have a pan on the stove, the heat from the stove spreads through the pan. If you take the pan off the stove, the pan cools. The heat flows into the air.

The work of inventors such as James Prescott Joule (1818–1889) helped test these laws. He was an English scientist whose experiments showed that motion creates heat. A unit of measurement—the **joule**—was named after him. One joule is about the amount of energy needed to quickly lift a small apple about 3 feet (1 meter) straight up.

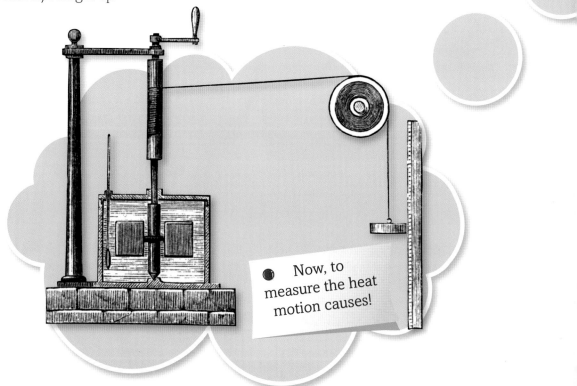

● Now, to measure the heat motion causes!

Meet Rudolf Clausius

Rudolf Clausius (1822–1888) was a German scientist and mathematician. He studied Earth's atmosphere to explain such things as why the sky is blue. Later, he turned his studies to heat. He helped explain natural laws related to heat. His major contributions reached beyond science. He organized an ambulance corps during the Franco-Prussian War in 1870. He was even wounded in a battle. He also raised his large family after his wife died while giving birth to the last of their six children.

Make a Sound Machine

You Will Need:

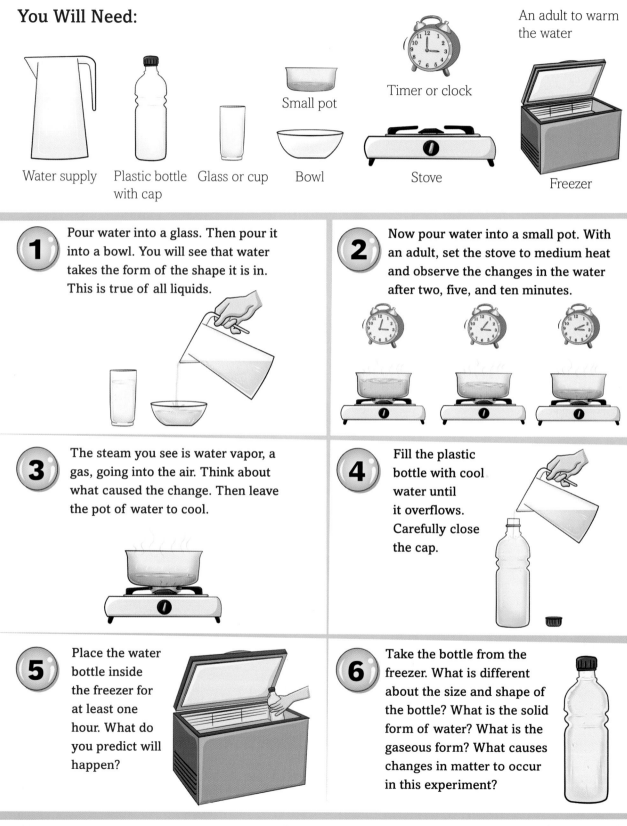

Water supply

Plastic bottle with cap

Glass or cup

Bowl

Small pot

Timer or clock

Stove

An adult to warm the water

Freezer

1 Pour water into a glass. Then pour it into a bowl. You will see that water takes the form of the shape it is in. This is true of all liquids.

2 Now pour water into a small pot. With an adult, set the stove to medium heat and observe the changes in the water after two, five, and ten minutes.

3 The steam you see is water vapor, a gas, going into the air. Think about what caused the change. Then leave the pot of water to cool.

4 Fill the plastic bottle with cool water until it overflows. Carefully close the cap.

5 Place the water bottle inside the freezer for at least one hour. What do you predict will happen?

6 Take the bottle from the freezer. What is different about the size and shape of the bottle? What is the solid form of water? What is the gaseous form? What causes changes in matter to occur in this experiment?

WHO WOULD HAVE THOUGHT?

When ice melts and turns to water, is there a change in temperature? Actually, there's a change in heat. Heat goes into the solid, and the solid melts. When a substance like water changes from one state to another, we say it undergoes a **phase change**. The three states of matter are solid, liquid, and gas. Phase changes happen because of a change in heat. Heat either goes into or leaves a material, causing the phase change. When a liquid freezes, heat leaves the liquid. The liquid becomes a solid. Where does the heat go when a liquid changes into a gas? Heat goes into the liquid.

How Does Heat Move?

Conduction, convection, and radiation all transfer heat. Usually heat moves from objects of higher temperatures to objects of lower temperatures. Some kinds of heat transfer happen naturally, such as when the Sun warms a car hood. Other times, we control heat transfer for special purposes. A refrigerator transfers heat so we can keep food cool. Air conditioning and furnaces transfer heat so we can stay cool on hot days and warm when it's cold outside.

Many inventors have used the laws of heat to make items that help in everyday life. Some of these inventors stand out, such as the African-American inventor David Crosthwait (1898–1976). He designed heating and cooling installations. He held more than thirty-nine U.S. **patents** for his work with heating systems, **vacuum pumps**, and refrigerators.

Crosthwait wrote a manual on heating and cooling with water, as well as a number of other guides. He designed the heating system for two famous buildings in New York City: Radio City Music Hall and Rockefeller Center.

The **problem of heating** and **cooling** large buildings is a real challenge. Each building is different. So each solution is different.

Meet Frederick McKinley Jones

Frederick McKinley Jones (1892–1961) was another African-American inventor. He patented more than sixty inventions having to do with heating and air conditioning. He taught himself all about electronic devices. When he was first hired to work at a garage, his job was sweeping and cleaning. Jones watched mechanics working on cars, and within three years he was in charge of the garage. His fascination with motors grew, and he became a great inventor.

How Do You Keep An Ice Cube From Melting?

You Will Need:

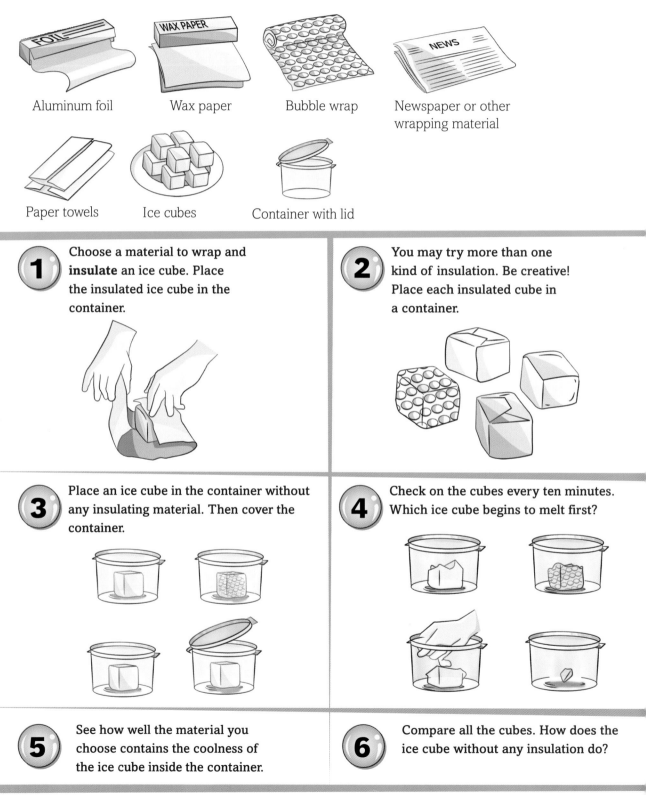

Aluminum foil

Wax paper

Bubble wrap

Newspaper or other wrapping material

Paper towels

Ice cubes

Container with lid

1 Choose a material to wrap and **insulate** an ice cube. Place the insulated ice cube in the container.

2 You may try more than one kind of insulation. Be creative! Place each insulated cube in a container.

3 Place an ice cube in the container without any insulating material. Then cover the container.

4 Check on the cubes every ten minutes. Which ice cube begins to melt first?

5 See how well the material you choose contains the coolness of the ice cube inside the container.

6 Compare all the cubes. How does the ice cube without any insulation do?

WHO WOULD HAVE THOUGHT?

Sometimes ideas come from unexpected places. Frederick Jones talked with a truck driver who had suffered a loss. The storage space in the driver's truck had overheated, and the chickens he was carrying had died from the heat. The story inspired Jones to invent a refrigeration system for trucks and railroad cars. Called the Thermo King, his invention ended the risk of food spoiling. During World War II, this invention saved lives. Jones's company made a small refrigerator unit that carried **blood plasma** to troops in the field. It could be used to take the plasma behind enemy lines.

Heat Is All Around You

When you pay attention to the world, you will find many kinds of heat and almost as many ways that heat can be formed. Here are just a few types of heat all around you!

Geothermal energy: Have you wondered what happens deep inside Earth? Geothermal energy is energy generated in Earth's core, about four thousand miles below the surface. The steam and hot water created there can heat buildings and generate electricity. If you see a **geyser** erupt, perhaps you are seeing thermal energy at work. That super-heated water comes from deep inside Earth.

Friction: Friction is the rubbing of two things together. Try rubbing your hands together. Can you feel the heat? Friction causes heat. Rubbing two things with rougher surfaces makes more heat than rubbing things with smooth surfaces. Try rubbing different types of surfaces together to see the differences in heat.

Meet John Herschel

John Herschel (1792–1871) was a well-known astronomer. A crater on the moon was named after him. He even figured out an early way to use solar energy. Long before there were solar panels heating buildings, he was using a solar box. During a trip to Africa in the 1830s, Herschel collected heat from the Sun with a solar thermal collector box. He used this box to cook his food.

Let's not forget **solar energy!**

The Sun has produced energy for billions of years.

The Sun's rays that reach Earth create solar energy.

Solar energy can be turned into other kinds of energy, such as heat and electricity.

Solar energy is **renewable**—we can get more!

Experiment with SONAR

You Will Need:

Water

Aluminum can

3 squares of cardboard, about 12 inches long and wide

Aluminum foil

Sun

1 Cover one side of each of the cardboard pieces with foil.

2 Set up the cardboard-covered foil in full sun. Place one piece of cardboard, foil side up, as the bottom.

3 Place the other two pieces of cardboard, foil side inward, so that all three pieces are in direct sun. Fill the can with water.

4 Place the can inside the cooker.

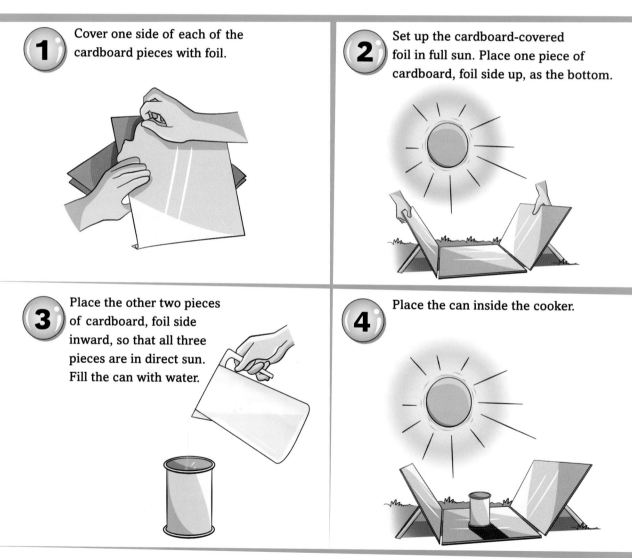

5 Check the temperature of the water with your finger every fifteen minutes. Sunlight is energy that heats the cooker.

WHO WOULD HAVE THOUGHT?

Can you picture Benjamin Franklin standing in a thunderstorm with a kite and a key? As John Herschel is known for astronomy, Franklin is known for his work with electricity. Yet both worked with heat. In colonial America, severe winters made homes cold. People often built open fires inside, which was dangerous. Franklin invented an iron furnace stove, now known as the Franklin stove. The stove drew in cool air, heated it, and then **circulated** it. It is yet another example of how inventors have made lives better by thinking about the problems around them and coming up with solutions.

Timeline

1714
Daniel Fahrenheit invents the modern thermometer, using mercury.

1724
Fahrenheit introduces his temperature scale.

1742
Anders Celsius invents the Celsius temperature scale.

1742
Benjamin Franklin invents the Franklin stove, a safer method of heating homes.

1798
Ben Thompson presents his theory that heat is produced by the motion of particles.

1830s
John Herschel uses a solar box cooker.

1850
Rudolph Clausius states that heat cannot pass from a colder body to a hotter body.

1848
Lord Kelvin invents the Kelvin temperature scale.

1920
David Crosthwait patents a device that returns heat to a boiler, one of 39 U.S. patents he will get in his lifetime.

1843
Joule discovers an important law about how heat acts.

1938
Frederick McKinley Jones gets the idea for the Thermo King.

1841
James Prescott Joule shows that energy is conserved in electrical circuits.

Glossary

absorb To take in or swallow up.

atmosphere All the layers of air around Earth.

atom The smallest particle of an element that has all the properties of that element.

blood plasma The watery part of blood that transports blood cells.

circulated Moved in a circle or around a course, returning to the same point.

concrete Building material that mixes cement, sand, gravel, and water.

conduction Transfer of heat from one substance to another through direct contact.

convection Transfer of heat in a gas or a liquid by particles moving within the fluid.

entropy Measure of disorder in a system.

friction Resistance made as one object moves over another object with pressure.

geothermal energy Energy from the heat inside Earth, usually carried to the surface by superheated water and steam.

geyser Spring in the ground that can sometimes shoot hot water.

heat A form of energy created by the movement of molecule, atoms, and smaller particles of matter.

insulate To cover with material that stops energy such as heat from getting in or out.

joule A unit of energy; the amount of energy it would take to send something that weighs one kilogram one meter up per second.

molecule The smallest particle of an element that still has the characteristics of the element.

particle Small piece; a tiny bit of something.

patent Document issued by the government that gives an inventor rights to an idea.

phase change Change in a physical state of a substance from solid to liquid, liquid to gas, or solid to gas, or the reverse.

radiation Energy that moves from a central source in the form of rays, waves, or particles.

reflect To bend or throw back waves of light, heat, or sound.

renewable Can be fully supplied or replaced naturally.

solar energy Energy produced from the Sun's radiation.

temperature Degree of hotness or coldness of a body or environment as shown by a thermometer.

theory Idea or plan of how something might happen or be done.

thermodynamics Relationship between heat and other properties, such as temperature or pressure.

thermometer Instrument for measuring temperature.

transfer To move from one place or situation to another.

vacuum pump Machine that draws gas or air out of a sealed space.

Index